SUPERHERO SIBLINGS

By Kaylonni Isis Turner

Copyright © 2022 by Kaylonni Isis Turner.

All rights reserved. No part of this book may be reproduced or used in any manner without written permission of the copyright owners except for the use of quotations in a book review or for educational purposes.

ISBN: 978-1-7373993-2-2
Publisher: Isis Publishing, LLC.

Dedicated to my super cool, hilarious, creative, and intelligent superhero children; Nora, Liam, and Yara.

And to all of our children: may your creativity, imagination, and joy always illuminate your superpowers within.

"Liam, come on! It's a beautiful day. There's so much we can do. Let's go outside and play!"

Nora held the door as the siblings ran outside to play.
They jumped, laughed, and flipped.
They were ready for an adventurous Saturday.

They shouted hooray as they ran wild and free.
There was so much to do,
what would their next game be?

"I have an idea," Liam said. "Let's dig for treasure."
The siblings quickly grabbed their shovels.
They promised to work together.

On their hands and knees, each of them started to dig.
They went deeper and deeper, hoping to find something big.

"Nora! Liam! My shovel is stuck! Should we find out why? Maybe it's good luck!"

Nora, Liam, and Yara looked at each other with the biggest, brightest eyes. They opened the box to see what was inside.

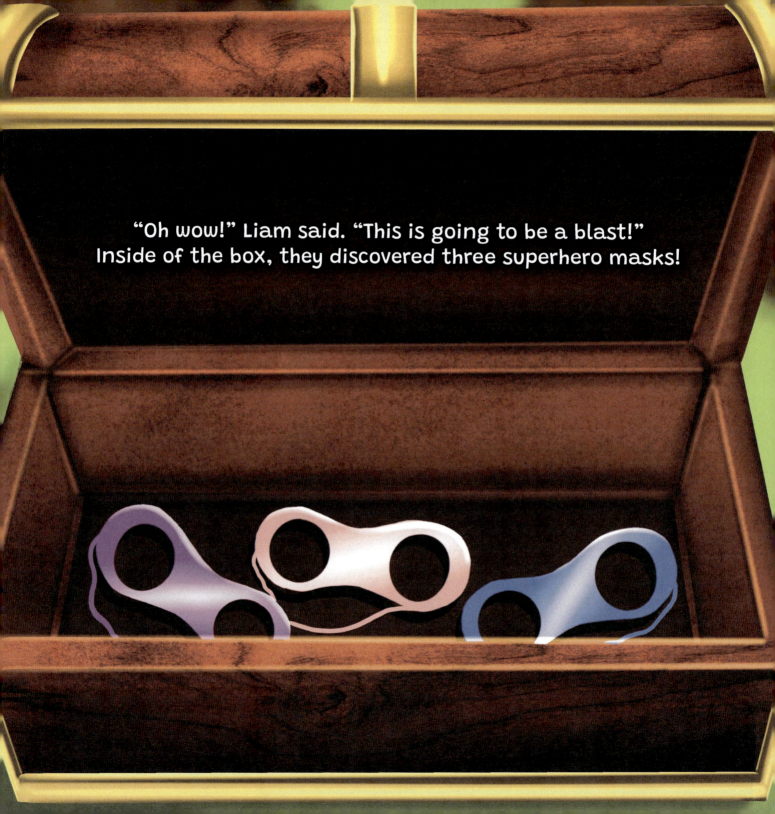
"Oh wow!" Liam said. "This is going to be a blast!"
Inside of the box, they discovered three superhero masks!

Nora's legs and feet sparkled like stars in the night sky.
The mask helped her move like a lightning bolt passing by.
She could run around the entire Earth in seconds with ease.
Her brand-new superpower was super speed!

Liam grew huge muscles. He was as solid as a tank. His brand-new superpower was super strength. He could lift anything, no matter how heavy. His power kept the siblings safe and steady.

Through the window, their parents watched their children outside. As the siblings showed off their superpowers, their mommy and daddy smiled with pride.

Their beautiful children had discovered something new. Nora, Liam, and Yara's superpowers made their big debut.

They had the superpowers and now they had the look.
It was time to save the world, no matter how long it took.

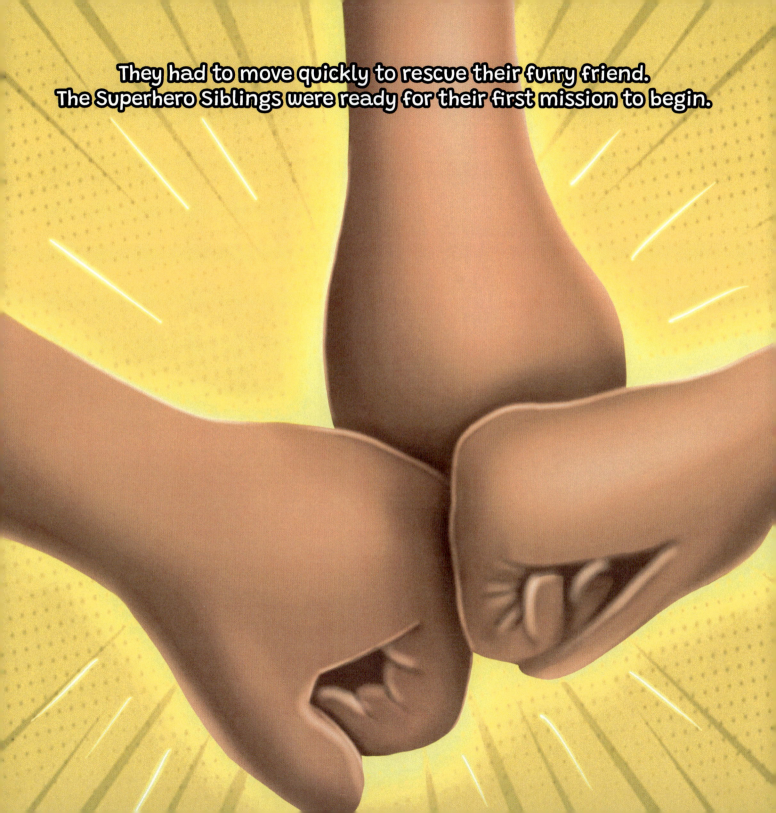

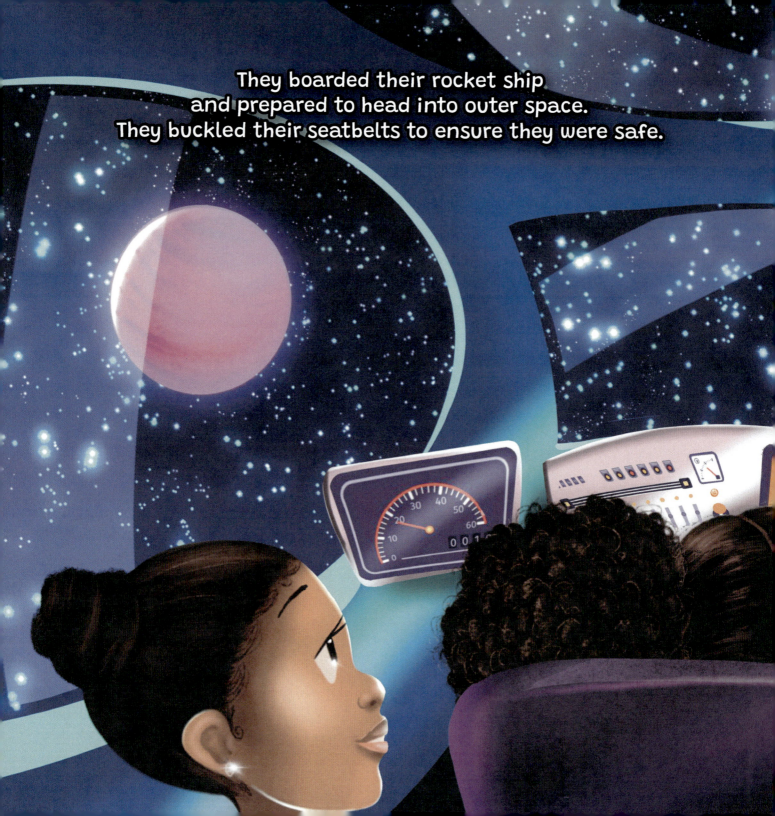

Before they could get to Blacky, they had to come up with a plan. They needed everyone's superpowers to conquer the task at hand.

First, they needed Yara to freeze the outer space goo. That way, they could ice skate to Blacky without getting stuck too.

Once they got to Blacky on the frozen solid goo, they needed Liam's super strength to break their furry friend loose.

When Blacky broke away from the ice, some acorns did too.
As the acorns floated away, Blacky chased after his favorite food.

Nora saw what was happening and put her super speed to use. She ran so fast that lightning bolts were coming from her boots.

She scooped Blacky up right before he reached the crack.
He was so happy the Superhero Siblings had his back.

They all boarded their spaceship and made their way back home to Earth. They were so excited, they felt like they would burst.

"Okay guys, we're finally home so you know what that means. We have to tell our parents about our superpowers. They are going to be so pleased!"

Nora, Liam, and Yara ran inside to share the big news. "We have superpowers and just saved Blacky on the moon!"

About the Author

Kaylonni Isis Turner is the Founder, CEO, and Author of Yara Klaire Book Series, LLC.

Her passion for reading and writing budded at the early age of seven as she would sit at the dining room table, drawing and writing stories about everywhere her vivid imagination would take her. Her natural love of writing led her to earn her Bachelor's Degree in Journalism from Michigan State University.

As a Wife and Mother of three adventurous toddlers who share her infatuation with reading, Kaylonni became inspired to write children's books when she saw the need for books that revolve around characters who her children could see themselves in.

Passionate about representation and inspired by her children, Kaylonni created Yara Klaire Book Series to uplift and inspire young, Black Children through positive affirmations, beautiful imagery, and exciting adventures with characters who look just like them.

To contact Kaylonni visit:
www.YaraKlaireBooks.com
Email: Contact@YaraKlaireBooks.com
Instagram: @YaraKlaireBooks
Facebook: **Yara Klaire Book Series (@YaraKlaireBooks)**

Made in the USA
Monee, IL
22 May 2023